FABULATION
OR, THE RE-EDUCATION OF UNDINE

BY LYNN NOTTAGE

DRAMATISTS
PLAY SERVICE
INC.

FABULATION OR, THE RE-EDUCATION OF UNDINE
Copyright © 2005, Lynn Nottage

All Rights Reserved

FABULATION OR, THE RE-EDUCATION OF UNDINE was originally produced by Playwrights Horizons (Tim Sanford, Artistic Director; Leslie Marcus, Managing Director; William Russo, General Manager) in New York City, opening on June 13, 2004. It was directed by Kate Whoriskey; the set design was by Walt Spangler; the costume design was by Kaye Voyce; the lighting design was by David Weiner; the sound design was by Ken Travis; and the stage manager was Gillian Duncan. The cast was as follows:

UNDINE	Charlayne Woodard
FLOW / ENSEMBLE	Daniel Breaker
MOTHER / ENSEMBLE	Saidah Arrika Ekulona
ACCOUNTANT / ENSEMBLE	Stephen Kunken
HERVÉ / GUY / ENSEMBLE	Robert Montano
STEPHIE / ENSEMBLE	Melle Powers
FATHER / ENSEMBLE	Keith Randolph Smith
GRANDMA / ENSEMBLE	Myra Lucretia Taylor

CHARACTERS

UNDINE

(Ensemble)

STEPHIE	DRUG DEALER
ACCOUNTANT RICHARD	OFFICER
AGENT DUVA	GUARDS
HERVÉ	INMATES
DOCTORS	ADDICTS
RAPPER	GUY
ALLISON	DEVORA
BABALAWO	ROSA
MOTHER	GREGORY
FATHER	CASE WORKER
FLOW	MOVERS
GRANDMA	WELFARE APPLICANTS
LANCE	YOUNG PREGNANT WOMAN

PLACE

New York City.

TIME

The present.

AUTHOR'S NOTE

The ensemble of four women and four men play multiple characters, with the exception of the actress playing Undine. The pace of the play should be rapid and fluid, allowing the scenes to blend seamlessly into each other without ever going to blackout until the end.

Suggested doubling:

Guy/Hervé/Lance

Accountant Richard/Addict #1/Mover/Applicant/Doctor #2

Stephie/Counsellor/Devora/Pregnant Woman/Applicant

Agent Duva/Flow/Rapper/Drug Dealer/Mover/Addict Ensemble/Applicant

Doctor Khdair/Grandma/Inmate #1/Case Worker

Allison/Mother/Rosa/Inmate #2/Addict Ensemble/Applicant

Babalawo/Father/Gregory/Applicant

FABULATION
OR,
THE RE-EDUCATION OF UNDINE

ACT ONE

Scene 1

Undine, thirty-seven, a smartly dressed African American woman, sits behind a large teak desk sporting a sleek telephone headset.

UNDINE. Can I be honest with you? I admire your expectations, but they're unrealistic, love. Yes, I can deliver something within your range. But your ambition outpaces your budget. But, but, listen to me, it's going to be a total waste of our energy. I've been doing this for a very long time. People give more when they get more, they want a seat next to a celebrity and a five-pound gift bag. It's the truth. Five years ago you could get away with half glasses of chardonnay and a musical theatre star, but not today. Generosity doesn't come cheaply. You're competing with heifers and amputees, rare palms and tuberculosis. What about the cause? Love, people don't want to think about a cause that's why they give. Yes, I want to hear your thoughts, I am listening. Listen, I'm at the outer limits of my time and so I'm going to ask you to speak more quickly. I will. Yes. We'll talk tomorrow about the new budget. Bye-bye. *(Undine hangs up and unfurls a pleased self-satisfied smile. She buzzes her assistant.)* Stephie, if Altrice calls back tell her I've left for the day. *(Excited.)* Oh and did Hervé call? Buzz me when he does. *(Undine climbs onto the edge of her desk.)* And sweet pea where are we with tonight's event? Oh God, don't tell me that. You know the rule: if you can't get a celebrity, get me someone celebrity-like. Wait, wait I don't understand what you're saying. Stop, stop, stop. Get in here. *(To Herself.)* Okay, now how difficult is it to find me someone who can make an entrance? *(Stephie, a spacy twenty-something, enters in a very very short light-blue fur mini-skirt.)* Jesus, how difficult is it? They can send probes to Mars, and I'm just asking for someone slightly fabulous.

STEPHIE. Like?

UNDINE. Like the fuck blonde with the perky nipples. You know the one. She's what's-his-name's girlfriend. The comedian. You know. Her!

STEPHIE. She's an alcoholic, Undine.

UNDINE. So? The photographers adore her —

STEPHIE. She got sloppy drunk at the Wild Life benefit and puked on the buffet table.

UNDINE. I don't care if she's an alcoholic. As long as she can hold it together long enough for a photo-op. After that she can swim to Taiwan in booze for all I care.

STEPHIE. But —

UNDINE. Tell her it's an open bar, that way she'll get there on time.

STEPHIE. It … it doesn't feel right.

UNDINE. Oh it doesn't feel right? Visualize a job behind a counter, okay? How does that feel? Yeah, I thought so.

STEPHIE. Why are you being such a harpy this morning? You're acting like, I don't know a —

UNDINE. An employer? Oh please, back to the list my little hater!

STEPHIE. I've been through the list like four times, I've called absolutely everyone.

UNDINE. What about the contingency list?

STEPHIE. Done.

UNDINE. What about —

STEPHIE. She's doing something with —

UNDINE. Fuck her, she hasn't had a movie in two years, two years and I'm offering her free publicity.

STEPHIE. Sorry, I spoke to her myself and she's like on some sort of spiritual —

UNDINE. God damn it, if I hear about one more celebrity on a spiritual journey I will, I will … It's okay, she's closed that door. Let her go. Let her go do her yoga thing, I don't care. So? How are we doing with our friends in the media?

STEPHIE. The perennial from WBAI and some intern from *Newsweek* confirmed, and everybody else is wait and see. Like, no one cares about Fallopian Blockage. It isn't exactly —

UNDINE. Hush! This is going to be fine. We're okay, we have plenty of time. Call George, tell him Undine is cashing in her favor. I need someone up and coming, young, hip. Hip-hop in fact. On the verge. Gangsterish enough to cause a stir, but not enough to cause a problem. And don't let him weasel out. I don't want New York *Times* Hag-fest photos. Fun, fun, fun. *Vibe, Vanity Fair.* The V's. Let's mix and match a little bit, shake it up. Mix and match. Goddamnit if we can't find a celebrity we'll create a new one. This is going to be great. What are you wearing? Goodbye!

STEPHIE. But —

UNDINE. Goodbye! *(Stephie moves to leave, then remembers something.)*

STEPHIE. Oh I forgot, your accountant's waiting outside.

UNDINE. Oh God. What does he want? Give me a minute. *(Stephie leaves. Undine weeps uncontrollably. She stops abruptly, takes out a mirror, reapplies her lipstick, checks her teeth and wipes away the tears. Intercom.)* Send the little pussy in. *(Richard, an elegantly clad man in his mid-thirties, enters, shaking his head ever so slightly. All charm.)* Richard. Oh come on, it's little early in the day for a visit. Put away your business-school face. I'm not signing anything —

ACCOUNTANT. Why didn't you tell me you and Hervé split?

UNDINE. Why? Because I only just found out. Apparently I was the last to know.

ACCOUNTANT. Jesus, I'm sorry, Undine —

UNDINE. You? *(A moment.)* How do you think I felt when I woke up this morning and his closet was bare?

ACCOUNTANT. Yikes, how'd he manage that?

UNDINE. I don't know, he took clothing to the dry cleaners every day. I didn't question it. I just thought he had a compulsion to be clean. Little ferret. How was I to know that he was slowly sneaking out of my life, piece by piece.

ACCOUNTANT. Do you know where he is?

UNDINE. Uh ... No, and frankly I don't care.

ACCOUNTANT. Well, I wish you did.

UNDINE. We had dinner last night. I mean, we talked about redoing the living room in Antique White. Stupid, fucker. He was actually attentive and warm —

ACCOUNTANT. *(Blurts out.)* And he was, well, he ... Oooo ...

9

he was also slowly siphoning money out of your accounts. *(A moment.)*

UNDINE. *(Intercom.)* Stephie, would you come back in?

ACCOUNTANT. Undine, did you hear what I said? *(Stephie reenters.)*

UNDINE. Sweet pea, will you have Jeremy run out and buy me some aspirin, a pregnancy test kit. I also need a pair of panty hose, and tell that idiot that I don't wear flesh tone or natural. I'm suntan or bronzed or cocoa. Oh yes, and I desperately need a triple café latte, no milk.

STEPHIE. You mean a *(With an Italian accent.)* triple espresso.

UNDINE. I'm so pleased you learned something during your year in Italia. How much did that word cost your parents, five hundred dollars? But what I'm asking for is a triple café latte with no milk. Is that clear?

STEPHIE. Are you all right?

UNDINE. I'm waiting for my coffee. Pronto. That's Italian for do your job!

STEPHIE. Is there anything else?

UNDINE. Stephie.

STEPHIE. Yes?

UNDINE. I love you. Goodbye. *(Stephie leaves.)*

RICHARD. Undine, did you hear —

UNDINE. You're not saying that Hervé?

ACCOUNTANT. Has disappeared with —

UNDINE. I don't believe it. He's a duplicitous conniving prick, but he's not a thief. Lighten up, he probably just took a cruise to Saint Martins or moved the money into some mutual fund. He'll resurface when he gets bored. *(Richard laughs.)*

ACCOUNTANT. Saint Martins? I see. Shall I break it down? When you made your husband a co-signatory on all of your accounts, you essentially gave him the power to do whatever he wanted with your money. Which is exactly what has been done.

UNDINE. I'm sorry, my mind just went totally blank for a moment. Come again.

ACCOUNTANT. Undine, do you understand what I'm saying? He's absconded with all of your money.

UNDINE. Absconded? That's a very British word, Richard. You make it sound as if he's not coming back. *(Undine begins to laugh. Stephie reenters.)*

ACCOUNTANT. I'm dead serious. *(Undine stops laughing.)*

UNDINE. *(To Stephie, curtly.)* What?

STEPHIE. I have the caterer on line one.

UNDINE. And?

STEPHIE. Your credit card, like, didn't go through. Sorry.

UNDINE. *(Yells.)* Sweet pea, I can't deal with this right now! Make it work.

STEPHIE. But —

UNDINE. Richard, how much are we talking about?

ACCOUNTANT. A lot.

UNDINE. How much?

ACCOUNTANT. A lot.

UNDINE. What's left?

ACCOUNTANT. Um ... *(Accountant shuffles some papers.)* Nothing.

STEPHIE. Uh, the caterer's on the phone, um, like, she really needs to speak to you, what should I tell her? *(Richard lights a cigarette. Undine stands and paces.)*

UNDINE. Goddamnit, why didn't you do something?

ACCOUNTANT. He's your husband. I did what you asked. I didn't want to step —

UNDINE. But you're my accountant. I mean you've had dinner in my home, I bought a fucking five-thousand-dollar table to your wife's Blossom Buddy charity benefit. Good lord, I think we even got drunk once and made love in the men's room at Nell's. *(Stephie lets out a little gasp. Undine and Richard look away from each other.)*

ACCOUNTANT. Um, I know the timing is awful but, Undine, we're going to have to consider bankruptcy. It's the only way to protect yourself. There isn't a stigma anymore.

UNDINE. No. No. No. I don't want to talk about bankruptcy. I've spent fourteen years building this company. And that implies that some how I failed. Let me tell you something Mr. Harvard M.B.A. My ancestors came shackled in wooden ships, crossed the Atlantic with nothing but memories! But I'll spare you my deprivation narrative. Let's just say their journey brought me here, their pain, their struggle established me behind this fine expensive teak desk. It is teak, a rare, strong and endangered wood. And now you want me to declare bankruptcy because that Argentine prick has run off with my money.

ACCOUNTANT. Well, yes.

UNDINE. I will do what it takes. I will beg and borrow, but damn it I'm not giving up my business. That's what I have, this is what I am. I will meet this month's bills, and take it from there —

ACCOUNTANT. It's not that simple.

UNDINE. All right, Richard, then make it simple.

ACCOUNTANT. You're broke, Undine, you're one month away from —

UNDINE. Goddamnit, don't say it. *(A man dressed in a plain blue suit enters.)*

STEPHIE. Excuse me, but there's —

UNDINE. Why am I just finding this out now?

ACCOUNTANT. *(Snaps.)* Because you don't return phone calls and you don't listen to your messages on your answering machine. The truth is you have not heard anything anyone else has said in years!

STEPHIE. Uh —

UNDINE. *(Annoyed beyond reason.)* What? What? What?

STEPHIE. There's a man who's been waiting —

ACCOUNTANT. Um, there is one other thing.

UNDINE. More?

ACCOUNTANT. Undine.

UNDINE. Who are you?

ACCOUNTANT. This is —

AGENT DUVA. Agent Duva from the Federal Bureau of Investigations.

ACCOUNTANT. He'd like, um —

AGENT DUVA. To ask you a few questions.

ACCOUNTANT. I'm sorry, but this is about a little more than a spring shopping spree.

AGENT DUVA. Undine Barnes Call-es?

UNDINE. Calles. Yes.

AGENT DUVA. Fraud.

UNDINE. What? *(Agent Duva dramatically pounds the desk.)*

AGENT DUVA. FRAUD! Perhaps you're familiar with the term identity fraud? We've been investigating your husband's activities for quite some time. I know this isn't easy for you, it never is. We will find him, I promise. But beg my pardon for saying, there is one thing that troubles us about this … matter. Mrs. Calles, we've thoroughly searched our files, but our investigation can find no record of your existence prior to fourteen years ago. Undine Barnes Call-es, you seem to have materialized from the ether. We are not quite sure who you are.

UNDINE. Give me a moment. Please. That means step outside.

ACCOUNTANT, AGENT DUVA and STEPHIE. Of course. *(Accountant, Stephie and FBI Agent slip out. Undine lights a cigarette. Her right hand begins to shake slightly.)*

UNDINE. *(To audience.)* Actually, this is where the story will begin. It is mid-thought, I know, but it is the beginning. In the next twenty seconds I will experience a pain in my chest so severe, that I've given it a short simple ugly name. Edna. Forgive me, I *am* Undine Barnes Calles. Yes. I left home at thirteen. I was a bright child. I won a competitive scholarship through a better chance program to an elite boarding school in New England. I subsequently acquired a taste for things my provincial Brooklyn upbringing could no longer provide. I went to Dartmouth College, met and mingled with people in a constructive way, built a list of friends that would prove valuable years down the line. And my family ... they tragically perished in a fire, at least that's what was reported in *Black Enterprise*. It was a misprint, but I nevertheless embraced it as the truth. Fourteen years ago, I opened my own very fierce boutique PR firm catering to the vanity and confusion of the African American nouveau riche. And all seemed complete when I met my husband Hervé at a much too fabulous New Year's Eve Party at a client's penthouse. Eleven months later we married. *(Hervé enters wearing a well-constructed suit, and nursing a cocktail.)* Two years later he had a green card. Why? He permitted me to travel in circles I'd only read about in *Vanity Fair*.

HERVÉ. *(With thick Argentine accent.)* Corfu, Milano, Barcelona, Rio.

UNDINE. He gave me flair and caché. What can I tell you, Hervé was dashing, lifted from some black and white film retrospective. He was a romantic. But before I introduce you to Hervé, I will now introduce you to Edna. *(Undine grabs her chest, gasping for air; her face contorts with pain and she collapses against her desk.)* Stephie! Stephie.

Scene 2

Doctor Khdair flicks on the light. Undine sits on the examining table. Dr. Khdair carefully examines the chart.

UNDINE. So. Am I dying?

DR. KHDAIR. No.

UNDINE. *(Snaps.)* What do you mean no?

DR. KHDAIR. I thought you'd be relieved. I consider that good news.

UNDINE. Doctor Khdair, a heart attack at thirty-seven is never good news.

DR. KHDAIR. Well, you haven't had a heart attack.

UNDINE. Oh? *(Lighting a cigarette.)* Then you won't mind if I smoke.

DOCTOR. Yes, actually I do. I wish you would stop. *(The doctor removes the cigarette from Undine's mouth.)*

UNDINE. Why? So I can live to a ripe old age like some demure grandmother, and face dementia, incontinence and a sagging ass. No thank you. I decided years ago never to view myself as a victim. Doctor, I'm thirty-seven, the world is crumbling, an early death seems merciful.

DOCTOR. My God, that's tragic.

UNDINE. No, tragic is a crack-addicted woman breast-feeding her child. I'm far from tragic, thank you. Can I stand up?

DOCTOR. No. Have you recently experienced any undue stress in your life?

UNDINE. Like? Like if my husband left me suddenly, embezzling all of my money, leaving me on the brink of financial and social ruin? *(Dr. Khdair laughs.)*

DOCTOR. You're very funny. Oh no, no, no I'm talking about pressure at the job, an upcoming deadline, an important speech.

UNDINE. Work is work.

DOCTOR. How much coffee have you had today?

UNDINE. I don't know three, maybe four cups. I don't know. Is it important?

DOCTOR. Well, yes. I believe you've suffered a severe anxiety attack. It's not uncommon.

UNDINE. Anxiety? Me? Oh no, I don't think so.

DOCTOR. And why not?

UNDINE. Anxiety happens to weepy people on television news magazines.

DOCTOR. Well, all of your tests came back normal. But there's one other thing Ms. Calles. I ran some routine tests and congratulations, you're pregnant. *(A moment.)*

UNDINE. Pregnant? *(To audience.)* I met Hervé at a dinner party

14

three years ago. He was standing by the crudités dipping broccoli spears into the dip. *(Hervé enters. He wears a well-constructed suit, he moves with the grace of a flamenco dancer. He holds a broccoli spear between his fingers.)* He did it with such flair that I found myself hovering around the hors d'oeuvres table for most of the evening. I watched, dazzled, as he sucked the dill dip off the vegetable with his full lips. *(He pops the broccoli spear into his mouth and wipes his lips with a napkin.)* Up until then I'd been dating a rapper at the twilight of his career. *(Rapper Boyfriend enters.)* He'd become addicted to pain-killers and his paranoia was making the relationship tiresome, he'd drive around Bushwick, Brooklyn, in his SUV, tunes pumping, yearning for ghetto authenticity. His six-figure income had isolated him from the folks. But nevertheless, he was becoming more ghetto by the moment. Too ghetto for the ghetto. *(Hervé gazes at Undine; their eyes lock.)* Hervé looked over at me, I was five, I was twelve, I was seventeen, I was twenty-eight. I explored the full range of my sexual awakening in that moment. As he approached I could not move my feet, and actually felt something I read a million times in romance novels, a tingle in my loins.

HERVÉ. *(With thick Argentine accent.)* Hello.

UNDINE. Hello. Did you enjoy the dip? *(To audience.)* I could think of nothing cleverer to say and averted my gaze. Then I glanced at my boyfriend with the hostess and a Philly blunt between his fingers. And I channeled all the charm in the universe. *(To Hervé.)* It is almost midnight and I see that you're alone.

HERVÉ. Yes, it appears so. *(A slow tango begins to play.)*

UNDINE. Have you seen the view from the balcony? It is spectacular.

HERVÉ. Yes … I have … seen … the view, and it is spectacular. Could I interest you in a dance? *(Hervé extends his hand. He pulls Undine in close.)*

UNDINE. *(Breathless.)* What is this music?

HERVÉ. You have never heard of Andres Segovia?

UNDINE. No. *(They begin to Tango.)*

HERVÉ. *Por que?* He is a master of classical guitar from *España*. The best, of course. He found a way to isolate emotion with his fingers. *(Hervé leads Undine through a series of elaborate dance steps.)* What he can do with a series of chords … is remarkable. I fell in love with his music in Madrid. I was curating an exhibition of important artists in *España*. I had the good fortune of dining in a café with the brilliant artist Ernesto Perez. The music began. The guitar. A recording of

Segovia's music. The place fell silent. We listened, intensely, for with a mere guitar he created an orchestra, indeed from those most basic chords he wove something so marvelously complicated, that it made us ashamed of our own limitations. In that small cafe Segovia opened up possibility. *Querida,* I can't believe you don't know his music. *(The music ends. Hervé kisses her hand.)*

UNDINE. *(To audience.)* And with a handful of words, I had fallen in love. *(Hervé exits.)*

Scene 3

Undine's office. Allison, a well-turned-out African-American woman, enters with two glasses and a bottle of wine. She speaks with an affected pseudo-upper-class British accent and carries herself with great poise and self-importance. Actually, she struts.

ALLISON. Did you tell him? Does he know?

UNDINE. No. *(Allison sits on Undine's teak desk.)*

ALLISON. What are you going to do?

UNDINE. Exercise my constitutional right.

ALLISON. He doesn't deserve to be a father —

UNDINE. Or a husband —

ALLISON. Bastard —

UNDINE. Oh God, why did I have to get pregnant?

ALLISON. Don't speak to me about fertility. Look at me, I'm on hormone cocktails, and it is hideous.

UNDINE. But you don't want a child, Allison.

ALLISON. Of course I don't, but everyone else is doing it and you know Daryl, he won't be left behind. *(Allison unfolds the* Daily News, *and holds it out to Undine.)* Here. I brought you the *Daily News.* Page four. I thought you might —

UNDINE. I have it —

ALLISON. Did you see the photo that they used?

UNDINE. No kidding.

ALLISON. Terrible. You're not that heavy, darling.

UNDINE. Fraud! Can you believe that Argentine testicle was breaking the law on my nickel?

ALLISON. Don't talk to me about it. I've been there with Daryl and the whole brokerage house scandal. Page two, three days running. I don't want to relive those years. I had to scratch and claw my way back onto party lists and even now around Christmas the mailbox isn't nearly as full. There is nothing less forgiving than Bourgie Negroes.

UNDINE. Who are you telling? My phone has stopped ringing. I even called the phone company to see whether it had been disconnected. I've become some sort of social pariah, people act as if the mere presence of my voice on an answering machine is enough to sully their reputation. I've called everyone in my rolodex. Diane Madison, Ken Brooks, Sylvia Foster-McKay.

ALLISON. Sylvia? *(Movers enter and throughout the rest of the scene they slowly disassemble Undine's office.)*

UNDINE. Yes. Most people never got back to me, and those that did seemed frightened by my predicament. Jesus Christ, you're the only friend who's bothered to visit.

ALLISON. *(Surprised.)* Is that so?

UNDINE. Uh-huh. No one seems troubled by the actual charges against me. No, the crime isn't being a criminal, it's being broke. It's apparently against the law to be a poor black woman in New York City.

ALLISON. *(Shocked.)* You're broke, darling? You didn't tell me that. *(Allison is truly disturbed by this revelation.)*

UNDINE. Yes. *(Whispered.)* They auctioned off my furniture; it was like a feeding frenzy, people I knew bidding on my possessions waving little flags and purchasing bits and pieces of my life for a bargain.

ALLISON. Vultures.

UNDINE. At some point I thought they were actually going to put me up on the block and sell me to the highest bidder. And in a flash I thought, "Thank God I got my teeth done last year." "Look at them teeth, she got a fine set of teeth y'all." How naïve, foolish of me to assume that I was worthy of some comfort and good fortune, a better chance. They give you a taste, "How ya like it?" then promptly take it away. "Oh I'm sorry we've reached our quota of Negroes in the privileged class, unfortunately we're bumping you down to working class." Working. I'm not even working. I think I'm officially part of the underclass. Penniless. I've returned to my original Negro state, karmic retribution for feeling a bit too pleased with my life.

ALLISON. Enough! This talk is unsettling me. I need a glass of wine. *(Allison pours them each a glass of wine.)*

UNDINE. I'm sorry, Allison. I didn't mean to burden you with all of this. I'm really glad you came. *(Undine takes in her empty office.)* This is it, a lifetime of hard work. And here I am on the verge of becoming a statistic. I don't want to raise a child by myself. Not like this. Fuck him! I took vows. Two years, ten months and twelve days.

ALLISON. You could always marry that client of yours, the rapper, what's his name? Mo'Dough.

UNDINE. Yeah, and be a gangster bitch, a chicken head, no thank you. The money wouldn't last, and really is there anything more pathetic than an aging broke b-boy who ain't got no rap left.

ALLISON. Then what you are you going to do?

UNDINE. I don't know! Don't ask me. Maybe I'll go to church or give alms. I'll climb a mountain or tend to some limbless African children in the middle of a malaria zone. *(They share a laugh at the notion.)* And by the way, when did you acquire that fabulous walk?

ALLISON. Do you like it?

UNDINE. Yes. I love it.

ALLISON. Good. I've been trying it out. I'm in my Eartha Kitt phase, I'm making bold social choices. You don't think it's too much?

UNDINE. Of course it is. But you do your thing, girl. *(To audience.)* Allison, known in Harlem as Tameka Jo Greene, aspired to the Black bourgeoisie after a family trip to New Rochelle. She managed to transcend her modest childhood in the Langston Hughes public houses. Yes, a member of a Hundred Black Women, owns a house on Martha's Vineyard, an apartment on the Upper East Side, the low seventies. Then her husband appeared naked in a gay porn magazine, and the youthful indiscretion stripped her of her social status. But I admire her tenacity. It is an unrelenting struggle to regain social favor. And God bless her, she's on hormones and on the verge of a re-emergence.

ALLISON. I'm your best friend. Whatever you need, I'm here.

UNDINE. I have to move out of my apartment. May I stay with —

ALLISON. *(Dropping all affect.)* Oh Girl, we'd love to have you, but you know, we're in the process of renovating. It's absolutely crazy. *(Restoring the affect.)* Listen, we have the new place on the Vineyard. You're welcome.

UNDINE. Thank you, but I can't leave New York, at least not until the investigation is complete —

ALLISON. My goodness, look at the time.

UNDINE. You have to leave so soon?

ALLISON. I'm having lunch with … Sylvia.

UNDINE. Sylvia?

ALLISON. Yes, but we'll have dinner soon.

UNDINE. Soon.

ALLISON. Promise.

UNDINE. Promise. *(Allison heads for the door, she stops herself.)*

ALLISON. Undine, you understand. *(Allison exits. A Yoruba Priest, dressed in white, enters carrying a candle and a Nigerian divination board.)*

YORUBA PRIEST. The spirits are speaking. The door to all roads is open.

UNDINE. *(To audience.)* Richard, my accountant, recommended I see a Yoruba priest. It was his parting advice on coping with my predicament. They were roommates at Harvard Business School. So I thought, why not? *(The Yoruba Priest throws out a handful of cowrie shells on a divination board.)*

YORUBA PRIEST. It seems you've angered Elegba. The keeper of the gate, he opens the doors to the spiritual world. He's one of the trickiest and most cunning *orishas*.

UNDINE. Okay, so what does that mean?

YORUBA PRIEST. He's quite furious from what I see here.

UNDINE. Why on earth is Elegba angry at me? What have I ever done to the African spirits? *(The Yoruba Priest throws out a handful of cowrie shells on a divination board.)*

YORUBA PRIEST. *(Surprised and concerned.)* Oh?

UNDINE. What? What do you see?

YORUBA PRIEST. It's what I thought. You have a bit of work to do in order to placate Elegba.

UNDINE. Work? Like what?

YORUBA PRIEST. He says it's been a long time since you've been home. And as such you must give him a thousand dollara and a bottle of Mount Gay premium rum.

UNDINE. What? You gotta be kidding. That's — *(Undine examines the cowries.)*

YORUBA PRIEST. Oh no. He's one of the most unpredictable and demanding orishas. It's a symbolic offering, an appeasement. But —

UNDINE. Will he accept a heartfelt apology? I mean, really, what is Elegba going to do with a thousand dollars?

YORUBA PRIEST. I don't ask, I interpret. But I've experienced his wrath and believe me if I were you, I'd pay the spirit.

UNDINE. Will he take a check? *(The Yoruba Priest throws out the*

cowrie shells, reads the configuration.)
YORUBA PRIEST. No. Cash only. Kneel and repeat after me.
Elegba, open this door — *(Undine kneels next to the Yoruba Priest.
He passes Undine a cigar.)*
UNDINE. *(To audience.)* I am taking no chances. *Ashé.* I lay my
last thousand dollars at the altar of an angry African spirit, light a
candle, smoke a Macanudo and on the advice of a spirit I reluc-
tantly return to my last known address in Brooklyn. *(Lights crossfade to a dining room.)*

Scene 4

*Walt Whitman projects. Undine's family. Mother, Father and
Grandma are straightforward no-nonsense people. Her brother, Flow, is a hipster with a tatty Afro and goatee and has the
habit of speaking a bit too loudly. They all wear security guard
uniforms, except Grandma, who wears a brightly colored
Conway housecoat. Grandma, regrettably, is confined to a
wheelchair. The family sits around the kitchen table without
speaking. Father places the* Daily News *on the table and takes
a long swig from a large can of beer.*

UNDINE. So, can I stay here until I get back on my feet?
MOTHER. Let me get this straight — you want to stay here?
Here?
UNDINE. Yes.
MOTHER. Oh. I suppose, we got the room. I … I … *(Silence.)*
UNDINE. It's all right for us to speak. *(A moment. Silence.)*
FLOW. So.
UNDINE. Yes?
FLOW. You bugged out.
MOTHER. Shhh. Your sister's come home for a little rest and
relaxation.
FLOW. What the fuck? Club Med was overbooked?
MOTHER. Shhh. Shhh.
FLOW. You ain't been here for years, and you just decided in to stop
in for a little R and R, forgive my skepticism and tone of disbelief.

20

I'm going to laugh real hard and long for moment. *(Flow bursts into laughter.)*

UNDINE. At least I left, Flow. Are you still working on the epic poem about Brer Rabbit?

FLOW. *(Suddenly serious, without a breath.)* It is the exploration of the African American's journey. I'm exploring the role of the trickster in American mythology. I am using Brer Rabbit, classic trickster, as means to express the dilemma faced by cultural stereotyping and the role it plays in the oppression on one hand and the liberation of the neo-Afric "to coin a phrase" individual, on the other. We at once reject and embrace —

UNDINE. *(To audience.)* Flow was never the same after his tour of Desert Storm. I know it's a cliché, but something did happen to him in the desert. Military school, a year at West Point, the Green Berets and finally a security guard at Walgreen's. He couldn't ever reconcile his love of the uniform with his quest for personal freedom. Hence the poem.

FLOW. It is this very conundrum that intrigues and confounds. We love, but we despise him. We admire, yet rebuke. We embrace, yet we push away. This glorious duality, enlivens and imprisons him. Because ain't he only hunting for "a way out of no way," as it's been said. And so you know, the poem is not about Brer Rabbit, he is merely a means to convey a truth

FATHER. Speak! *(Grandma nods off at the dinner table. Mother loses herself in a book of word search puzzles.)*

FLOW. It is open-ended. A work in progress. A continuous journey. Oh shit, what time is it? They just got in the new Epilady and all the little motherfucking thieves'll be in tonight. I gotta roll in ten.

MOTHER. So, how long are you going to be with us? *(Mother looks up from her word search.)*

UNDINE. I don't know.

MOTHER. Well, I hope you don't mind sharing the bed with Grandma. I'll turn the mattress before you go to sleep.

UNDINE. That's okay, I'll manage.

MOTHER. My God, look at you. *(The family cast their curious sorrowful eyes upon Undine.)*

UNDINE. No, don't look at me. Stop, looking at me. For God's sake. Will you all stop looking at me now. What? *(Silence.)* Hey. You've been quiet, Daddy, how have you been?

FATHER. Shit.

UNDINE. Excuse me?

21

FATHER. You know Velvet Whitehead dead.

MOTHER. What? *(Father pops open another can of beer.)*

UNDINE. Who's Velvet Whitehead?

FATHER. Snookie's cousin's brother's father. You know Velvet solved that mathematical problem yesterday. That equation they be talking about in the big paper. That problem all them scientists —

UNDINE. Mathematicians —

FATHER. — Been 'rassling with.

UNDINE. Yeah, right.

FATHER. Fifty-thousand-dollar award for solving it.

FLOW. What?

MOTHER. Velvet Whitehead?

FATHER. Yesterday. We was sitting up in Cellars restaurant and he said, "Let me see that shit." Yes, he did. It took the brother all of ten minutes, he wrote the solution out on a napkin.

FLOW. Smart brother. Did two years at Stony Brook.

FATHER. Read the New York *Times* every mutherfucking day, subscribed to *The Economist*. *The Economist*, that's a magazine from England.

UNDINE. Yes, I'm familiar with England, I've actually *(Affecting an English accent.)* been.

FATHER. You been to England?

FLOW. But she ain't been home.

FATHER. But our Velvet was an around-the-way brother. Real. You know, could talk some talk like he was theoretician and a minute later be bullshitting with some crazy-ass fool on the corner.

MOTHER. I bet Gloria is all torn up.

FATHER. Velvet saw the equation on the page, little printed x's and numbers and bam the solution revealed itself. It was a wonder to watch the brother work. His brain was like Coltrane on the sax, you know. *(Scats.)* 1, 2, 3, 7, 9, 6, 13. *(Scats like numbers are tumbling out of his mouth.)* He kept decades' worth of shit in his head, spreadsheets, numbers, birthdays, deaths, a statistical oasis. Yeah. He wrote out the solution like it was a phone number, drank down his beer, sucked the last bit of meat off his spare ribs and talked about he was going to step outside to smoke a cigarette. I picked up the napkin, and I saw it, jack. Little numbers and letters, written in perfect Catholic-school hand. We was laughing, 'cause we had already spent his fifty thousand dollars, when we heard the gunshot. BAM! By the time we ran outside Velvet was dead. A bullet to the right side of his head. Yeah, baby, they knocked his cerebellum clear out his skull, splattered onto the parking meter with ten minutes left. And I went back inside to call the ambulance and the waitress was wiping up the table with Velvet's solution. Easy come, easy go, baby.

UNDINE. I don't want to rain on your parade, but how do you know he really solved the problem?

FATHER. 'Cause he did. *(With intensity.)* He looked at it, jack … And I saw it in his gaze, it was there for him. Absolute clarity, understanding, calm. He talked about how white folks overcomplicate things by not seeing the beauty, the basic formula, the rhythm of life. I tell you, the solution was there as plain as the truth. It was the truth. And I believed him. They'll have us believe that the problem can't be solved, that it ain't even within our grasp. So a nigger don't even bother to reach. But there are brothers like Velvet all over this city. I met brothers in 'Nam that should have been generals, but left with an enlisted man's pension. That's what I'm talking about. Velvet solved that problem, baby. He solved it, as clearly as anyone will.

UNDINE. You're a trusting friend. A folded New York *Times* and some scribbles on a napkin, with such faith you'd think there'd be no more problems in the world.

FLOW. What do you know with your bootleg ideas?

UNDINE. I know a fifty-thousand-dollar problem isn't solved on a napkin. I know something isn't so because you want it to be so. I mean, I'm sorry to hear about Velvet, I am. But I didn't come all the way home to talk about him. *(A moment.)* How are you, Daddy?

FATHER. I is and sometimes I ain't. *(Father shrugs his shoulders.)*

UNDINE. *(To audience.)* My family. The fire victims. Mother and Father good hard-working people. They took the police exam six times back in the seventies, before they realized the city wasn't going to let them pass. They settled into a life as security guards at Long Island University, hence the uniforms. It is a safe home.

MOTHER. *(Circling the word.)* Relief. Look at that.

UNDINE. What are you working on, Mom?

MOTHER. Wordsearch. Just finished my third book this week.

FLOW. So where's the baby daddy? What he gots to say about all this?

UNDINE. Isn't it time for your jackass pill?

MOTHER. Will you two please? Stop it! We're happy to have you home, Sharona. You stay as long as you want. There's plenty of room.

UNDINE. Mom, it's Undine.

MOTHER. I forgot, Undine, you gonna have to be patient.

FLOW. Well, I ain' calling her Undine. If it was Akua or Nzingha, a proud African queen, I'd be down with it. But you are the only sister I know that gots to change her beautiful African name to a European brand.

UNDINE. Correct me if I'm wrong, but you weren't exactly born with the name Flow. So shut up. *(Grandma audibly exhales, and nods out.)* What's wrong with Grandma?

MOTHER. She's just a little tired. Sometimes she nods off, the diabetes is taking its toll.

UNDINE. *(Loudly.)* Are you all right, Grandma?

MOTHER. She's fine, just let her be. *(A moment. Undine's breathing becomes, labored.)*

UNDINE. *(To family.)* Excuse me. I'm feeling a little nauseous. If you're going to the bathroom, take Grandma with you. *(The lights crossfade; we're now in Grandma's bedroom.)*

Scene 5

Grandma, all warmth and care, sits in her wheelchair crocheting a doily or something like that. Undine rests on the arm of the chair.

GRANDMA. You look good, Sharona.

UNDINE. I don't feel so.

GRANDMA. Been hoping you'd come home. I think about you a lot.

UNDINE. Nobody else seems particularly happy to have me back.

GRANDMA. Don't let them fool you, you they prize heifer. And sweet pea, you don't know how these folks brag on you.

UNDINE. I hope you don't mind that I'm sharing your room.

GRANDMA. Bet it ain't as beautiful as your apartment, but it got a lovely view of the next building. I've counted the number of bricks, 63,010 … What happened, Sharona?

UNDINE. It went away.

GRANDMA. Things don't just go away. They get taken away, they get driven away, they get thrown away.

24

UNDINE. All of the above.

GRANDMA. June seventeenth. It was an unseasonably cold day. You walked out that door in a dark-green linen suit, orange silk shirt and never walked back through, until now.

UNDINE. I had to. Mom opened the door, she pushed me towards it and I just stepped on through.

GRANDMA. It was a gentle nudge, not a push.

UNDINE. You didn't expect me to come back?

GRANDMA. A visit, yes.

UNDINE. You have been getting my Christmas cards?

GRANDMA. Your Christmas cards are always lovely. If they didn't come every year I'd think you fell off the earth.

UNDINE. I've been very busy. If you knew —

GRANDMA. A year I can forgive, but it has been nearly fourteen.

UNDINE. Fourteen? My God. Fourteen years. I really wasn't aware that that much time had passed. Honestly. Time just passed. It did.

GRANDMA. Are you ashamed of us?

UNDINE. No.

GRANDMA. But, you ain't telling the truth.

UNDINE. What do you want to hear? I was given an opportunity to get the hell out of here. And like anybody I took it. Isn't that what we all wanted? I just did it.

GRANDMA. Then why'd you come home?

UNDINE. I don't know what to say other than a month ago I sat in my doctor's office and she told me I wasn't dying and I was actually disappointed. I'm pregnant, Grandma, and I'm afraid that I'm not a good enough person to be a parent. So please I just want to sit here for a minute in silence and not have to freak out about my life. *(Grandma tenderly grasps Undine, but her hands begin to shake ever so lightly.)* What's wrong?

GRANDMA. Bad habits.

UNDINE. Are you all right, Grandma?

GRANDMA. Yes. No. Would you hand me that bag? I need my medicine. *(Undine lifts up a paper bag. The contents tumble out into Grandma's lap; a baggie of white powder, a box of matches, a hypodermic needle, a spoon and a tourniquet.)*

UNDINE. What is this?

GRANDMA. What it look like?

UNDINE. Is this stuff Flow's? Oh no, don't tell me he's using heroin.

GRANDMA. Why would you think that? Flow is trouble, but he

25

is a good man.

UNDINE. This belongs to somebody.

GRANDMA. I be that somebody.

UNDINE. You? *(Grandma's hand shakes as she rolls up her sleeve to reveal bruises lining her arm. She goes through the process of preparing the heroin. Horrified:)* Grandma, how long have you been shooting heroin?

GRANDMA. Since your grandfather died, baby girl.

UNDINE. Does Mommy know?

GRANDMA. If she do, she ain't said nothing.

UNDINE. I don't believe it.

GRANDMA. Pass me my works.

UNDINE. This is crazy.

GRANDMA. Change be what it will. I'd say it were crazy if it wasn't so necessary.

UNDINE. You nearly beat me down when you caught me smoking herb with Omar Padillo.

GRANDMA. Well, some things have happened since then. I got good and old for one. They think I'm diabetic. Your idiot brother even gives me the injections, my hands shake so bad these days.

UNDINE. I'm not going to watch you do this.

GRANDMA. I wish you wouldn't. *(Grandma tightens the tourniquet.)* Sweet pea, I thought that I'd get to this point and be filled with so much wisdom that I'd know just how to control the pain that's trailed me through life. The truth would be revealed, and some great doorway would open and God's light would encircle and lift me out of the ordinariness of my life. One would think you'd be closer to God at my age, but I find myself curiously further away.

UNDINE. How can you say that? You came up here with nothing. You got your high school diploma, worked two jobs and raised five beautiful children.

GRANDMA. Yes Lord. But, what do I get to look forward to each morning, the view of that brick building across the way and a perpetually gray life.

UNDINE. Stop it.

GRANDMA. For a few dollars I get to leave this drab apartment. Who is hurt? *(Emphatic.)* And I'm gonna die soon enough one way or the other. I'm old. I can't do it, Sharona. I ain't happy. At your age I already had five children. I did for others — so long, well, now it's time to do for myself. *(Grandma turns her back to Undine and injects herself with the heroin. She slips into a heroin induced languor, a junkie nod. She appears to be defying gravity as she leans forward in her chair. Just as she seems on the verge of falling out of the chair, she miraculously recovers. Undine watches, horrified, as her mother enters carrying a cup of hot chocolate.)*

MOTHER. I thought you might want some hot chocolate.

UNDINE. Do you know that Grandma is shooting heroin?

MOTHER. You always had an active imagination. *(Mother props Grandma up in the chair.)*

UNDINE. *(To audience.)* And this concludes the section entitled "Denial and Other Opiates."

MOTHER. She'll be all right, it's the sugar. *(Mother gives Grandma a kiss and exits.)*

UNDINE. Grandma, Grandma.

GRANDMA. Yes baby. Will you do me a favor?

UNDINE. Yes, of course.

GRANDMA. I need you to go out and get me some white lace.

UNDINE. What?

GRANDMA. My legs all swollen up, barely walk. But I'm gonna need another fix soon enough.

UNDINE. No, I'm not going to do it. I'm not. I refuse. No.

GRANDMA. You want me to die? That what you want? *(Shouts.)* I don't need no moralizing, I need smack and I need it now.

UNDINE. I don't even know where to get it.

GRANDMA. On the corner of —

UNDINE. *(To audience.)* One A.M. Saturday night. My entire life has been engineered to avoid this very moment. *(Undine sheepishly approaches a drug dealer lingering on the corner. She looks from side to side for some invisible jury.)* Excuse me.

DEALER. What?

UNDINE. I'd like one hundred dollars of *(Whispered.)* white trace please.

DEALER. What?

UNDINE. White taste. White lace, fuck, heroin!

DEALER. Do I know you?

UNDINE. No, and that's how I'd like to keep it.

DEALER. Are you a cop?

UNDINE. No. Are you a dealer?

DEALER. You sure you ain't a cop?

UNDINE. Would you like me to fill out a questionnaire? Let's cut the bullshit I'm not buying a condo. Just give me the God damn drugs — *(Undine thrusts the money in his direction.)*

DEALER. Bitch, put the money down, this ain't a fucking supermarket.

UNDINE. Listen friend this is humiliating enough without the insults. Can I give you a little business tip. If you treat your customers with respect, they'll give you a little respect in return.

DEALER. My customers are junkies, I ain't need they respect.

UNDINE. For the record, I'm not a junky.

DEALER. Oh you ain't a junky, you just copping dope for a friend.

UNDINE. Yes as a matter of fact.

DEALER. Bitch, give me the money. And get your tired junky ass out my face.

UNDINE. You call me bitch one more time and I just might take my business elsewhere.

DEALER. Take it elsewhere. Bitch!

UNDINE. My man, there is no need to resort to some ghetto drug dealer cliché. It's late, I'm not going to wander through this neighborhood looking for drugs, that's not my ideal Saturday evening out. So let's just wrap up this little interaction.

DEALER. Show me the dollars, and get the fuck out of here! *(Undine slips the dealer the money; he gives her the drugs.)* Ho! 5-0! *(Police sirens blare; the dealer tosses the heroin at Undine. A flashlight hits Undine, who freezes like a deer caught in the headlights. The dealer has already disappeared.)*

UNDINE. *(To audience.)* When you read the newspaper tomorrow and wonder, "How does it happen?" Now you know. One evening you're at a gala celebrating the opening of an expensive new museum wing and the next you're standing on a street corner with a hundred dollars worth of heroin and a flashlight shining in your face.

OFFICER. Arms where I can see them.

UNDINE. Officer, I know this may sound ridiculous, but this is not my heroin. I bought it for my grandmother.

OFFICER. State your name.

UNDINE. Undine Barnes Calles.

OFFICER. Do you have anything that's gonna stick me?

UNDINE. No.

OFFICER. Miss Calles, you have the right to remain silent. Anything — *(A photo is snapped. Camera flashes. Undine turns to the side. Camera flashes again. Undine is forcefully led to a prison cell occupied by two other women.)*

28

Scene 6

*Undine stands apart from the other women in the prison cell.
She steals a glance at Inmate #1, a hardened woman who
speaks in a harsh, biting tone.*

INMATE #1. Find what you looking for? *(Undine self-consciously
averts her gaze, and does not respond.)* You ain't hear me? Yeah, you.
UNDINE. Excuse me, are you talking to me?
INMATE #1. Who else I be talking to?
UNDINE. *(Under her breath.)* I don't know, Someone else, hopefully.
INMATE #1. What did you say?
UNDINE. Nothing.
INMATE #1. Don't make me have to come over there, and teach
you how to crawl. What, you think you special? There ain't no real
Gucci here. This the mark-down rack, bitch. *(Undine digs in her
bag and puts on a pair of dark Gucci sunglasses, and turns away.)*
Don't turn your head like I owe you money. Shit, you don't know
me. *(The woman laughs with bravado.)*
UNDINE. No.
INMATE #1. No, what?
UNDINE. No. I don't know you. And if I was looking at you, I
wasn't aware of it. I'm sorry.
INMATE #1. Oh, you sorry?
UNDINE. Yes, I'm sorry.
INMATE #1. That's right, you sorry.
UNDINE. Yes, I'm sorry. I'm sorry that I looked at you. Okay?
I'm sorry that you're so angry, I'm sorry that we're stuck here in the
middle of the fucking night. I'm sorry for a whole series of things
that are far too complicated to explain right now, and I'M SORRY,
THAT I'M SORRY. *(Unhinged.)* So if you don't mind, I'm going
to move to the other side of this … "cell" and sit quietly until they
call my name. If you want to hit me, hit me; otherwise back the
fuck off. *(Prison guard enters.)*
GUARD. Hey, hey. *(Undine, surprised by her own bravado, bursts
into tears. The sudden display of emotion catches Inmate #1 off guard,
and she backs off. The prison guard stares down Undine.)* What's

going on in here? Settle down. *(Inmate #2, quiet up until this point, edges toward Undine.)*

INMATE #2. Don't let her run over you, she born hard. She one of them prehistoric rocks been on the street too long. *(The prison guard continues to stare at Undine.)* Hey, sis, don't show him your tears. They get their strength from our pain. You cry the first time, you cry the second time, then the shit don't hurt so much after that. Suck it up. *(Undine gathers herself back up.)* What's your name, sis?

UNDINE. … Undine.

INMATE #2. That's a pretty name. For minute you looked like this stuck-up bitch who used to live in my building, but that diva wouldn't be caught dead here. *(Inmate #2 begins to laugh, Undine manages an ironic smile.)*

UNDINE. I'm not from —

INMATE #2. Your first time 'hoing?

UNDINE. NO! No. It was a misunderstanding. I don't really belong here —

INMATE #2. Guess what? I don't belong here, she don't belong here, but we here.

UNDINE. But you don't understand —

INMATE #2. Shit, all I was doing was buying formula for my cousin Leticia's baby over on Myrtle Avenue, right? And this dude, was you know, all up in my panties with his eyes. Right? On my shit like he my man. "You don't know me, brother," I told him. But he gonna get all pimp on me, like I's his bitch. Big fat Jay-Z–acting muthafucka. He think he all that 'cause he drivin' a Range Rover in my neighborhood. That don't impress me. Show me a pay stub, Brother. Show me a college diploma. But this dude is gonna step to my face. I told him, put your hands on me and see what happens.

UNDINE. And?

INMATE #2. Why you think I'm here? I showed the muthafucka the point of my heel and the ball of my fist. I told him, "I ain't your 'ho." "I work from 9 to 5 at Metrotech, my man, don't you look at me like a 'ho, don't you talk to me like a 'ho, don't you disrespect me like a video 'ho." Now, he gonna think twice 'fore he place a hand on another woman. Believe it. People think they know your history 'cause of what you wearing. Well guess what? I introduced him to Gloria Steinem with the back of my muthafucking hand.

INMATE #1. That's right. We don't got to take that shit!

UNDINE. They put you in here for that? It doesn't seem fair.

INMATE #2. Shit ain't fair. I mean, why are you here?

UNDINE. *(To audience.)* There is the question. I imagine the blurb in my college alumni magazine. Undine sends word from Rikers Island where she's enjoying creative writing and leading a prison prayer circle. *(Undine absorbs the horror of the question.)* Why are we here?

INMATE #2. You know what you done, you ain't gotta tell me. We do what we gots to do, right?

JUDGE HENDERSON. Undine Barnes Calles. Please step forward. The court of King's County, having found you guilty of the criminal possession of a controlled substance —

UNDINE. Your Honor —

JUDGE HENDERSON. — in the seventh degree, hereby sentences you to six months compulsory drug counseling.

UNDINE. But your Honor —

JUDGE HENDERSON. Failure to complete the program will result in a one-year jail sentence.

UNDINE. My God! *(Blackout.)*

End of Act One

ACT TWO

Scene 1

Lights rise on a semi-circle with a diverse collection of recovering drug addicts, who look to a sympathetic counselor for guidance. Undine, sipping a cup of coffee, is seated in the midst of semi-circle of addicts.

ADDICT #1. I miss it. I miss the taste and the smell of cocaine, that indescribable surge of confidence that fills the lungs. The numbness at the tip of my tongue, that sour metallic taste of really good blow. *(The addicts savor the moment. "Mmm.")* It was perfect, I mean in the middle of the day I'd excuse myself and slip out of an important faculty meeting, go to the stairwell and suck in fifteen, twenty, thirty dollars-worth of crack. *(The addict pretends to inhale. "Mmm.")* I'd return a few minutes later full of energy, ideas, inspired, and then go teach a course on early American literature and not give a God damn. In fact the students admired my bold, gutsy devil-may-care attitude. Why? Because I'd lecture brilliantly and passionately on books … I hadn't read. Indeed, the university didn't know how high and mighty I was when they promoted me chair of the English department and gave me an office with a view of Jersey. It was fantastic, I could smoke crack all day, every day in my office, seated in my leather chair, at my solid oak desk. It was near perfect, it was as close to nirvana as a junkie can achieve. But my colleagues were always on my case. "Beep, Mr. Logan wants you to attend a panel on the symbolism of the tomahawk in *The Deerslayer*. Beep, Beep, Ms. Cortini is here for her thesis defense, what should I tell her?" Those thesis writing mother fuckers drove me crazy. And I wanted to kill them. But, you know what happens I don't have to tell any of you junkies. "Beep, President Sayer wants to see you in his office. Right this minute. Beep. He's getting impatient." Fuck you! But by that time I was on a four-day binge, my corduroy blazer stank like Chinatown. And I was paraded through the hallowed halls like some pathetic cocaine poster child. But, I don't remember when I became a criminal, but it happened at some point after that. The descent was classic, it's not even worthy of detail. Bla, bla, bla. *(A moment. Guy, a gentle man, wearing a security guard uniform speaks up.)*

GUY. But you're clean, son. You're clear.

ADDICT #1. One year. One year clean and I still walk around the city wondering how people cope, how do they survive without the aid of some substance? A boost? It makes me angry, no envious. How come some people get to lead lives filled with meaning and happiness? And I become a drug-addled junkie scheming for my next fix.

ADDICT #2. Fuck them!

ADDICT#1. Excuse me, I didn't interrupt you. Thank you. And you know what I think? I think that they will never understand the joy and comfort of that very first moment you draw the smoke into your lungs releasing years of stress, of not giving a damn whether you live or die. They won't know what it is to crave and love something so deeply that you're willing to lie, cheat and steal to possess it. They won't know that kind of passion. I accept that I may go to hell, but I've experienced a kind of surrender, a letting go of self that years of meditation and expensive yuppie yoga classes won't yield. And I hold on to that feeling, fiendishly. That feeling empowers me, because I know the Shao-Lin strength that it takes to resist it, to fight it, to defeat it. *(A chorus of agreement rises up.)*

UNDINE. *(To audience.)* The perversity of this moment, is that in the midst of his loathsome confession, I'm actually finding myself strangely curious to smoke crack cocaine. I have now concluded that for every addict that the system cures two new ones are created. It is basic supply and demand, without the dependency on the system the system ceases to exist.

COUNSELOR. Undine, you've been sitting quietly, is there anything you want to share?

UNDINE. Other than the only meaningful contact I have these days is with the first sips of coffee in the morning. No. I'll just listen today.

COUNSELOR. You've been here five weeks. I think it might be helpful to open up.

ADDICTS. Open up, open up. *(The Addicts applaud in agreement.)*

UNDINE. *(To audience.)* Oh, to share my addictions. To confess to the stack of fashion magazines that I keep in my bathroom like some treasured porn collection, which I read and reread with utter salacious delight. No, I won't share that. Instead I manufacture some elaborate tale of addiction. I've decided to use Percodan as my gateway drug. And I concoct a tale so pathetically moving that I am touched by my own invention and regret not having experienced the emotions first hand. But the tears are genuine. I am crying. And I weep and I'm applauded by the room of addicts and it is exhilarating. A rush. And I understand addiction. *(Undine breaks down in tears. She is comforted by the addicts.)*

COUNSELOR. Remember this room is a safe haven. Whatever is spoken within this circle remains within the circle. And that trust is sacred as long as the circle is unbroken.

UNDINE. I'm pregnant and I don't know whether I want this child.

GUY. It is a blessing to be faced with such a dilemma.

UNDINE. What?

GUY. I said it's a blessing to be faced with such a dilemma.

UNDINE. Why?

GUY. A child, a possibility, a lesson.

UNDINE. *(To audience.)* He is speaking in sentence fragments and I find him curiously intriguing. *(To him.)* And?

GUY. 'Cause.

UNDINE. Yeah?

GUY. You know.

UNDINE. What?

GUY. A baby.

UNDINE. Yes.

GUY. Is a beautiful thing. *(Guy smiles.)* Not all of us have so perfect a reason to stay straight.

UNDINE. Oh my. You're right.

GUY. How long have you been using?

UNDINE. Long enough.

GUY. I've been clean for three years, it's my anniversary tonight and I'm trying to figure out how to celebrate. Will you have dinner with me?

UNDINE. Are you asking me out on a date?

GUY. Yes.

UNDINE. *(To audience.)* Dinner with a Junky? If I were a poet I would go home and compose a poem, threading the bits of irony through the improbability, but I'm not, so I say yes. BBQ on St. Marks and Second, a place I've shunned for a decade. He is reformed, he is magnificent and he is paying the bill. *(They sit side*

34

by side in the restaurant.)

GUY. I considered going into corrections, but a life of policing people behind bars seemed too, you know —

UNDINE. Depressing.

GUY. Yeah. It's like all my friends they either in jail, they on they way to jail or they the brothers watching the brothers in jail. I don't want that. It ain't part of my schedule. I'm clean, my head's like in the right place. I've been working at the Cineplex as a security guard, and I'm gonna take the firemen's exam next month.

UNDINE. A fireman, that's wonderful.

GUY. I got good upper body strength —

UNDINE. I bet you do.

GUY. And I can withstand really high temperatures, since I was eleven. It's one of those things. I'm studying in the evenings. And this time next year I'll be a fireman.

UNDINE. Really, I believe you will.

GUY. Yeah? You think so?

UNDINE. You know, I had my own business, a public relations firm, it started in a restaurant over a glass of wine. I had an expression very much like yours. I went from employee to entrepreneur between dinner and dessert. Really. *(Guy laughs.)*

GUY. I knew that about you. I knew that when you was sitting there quietly in counseling. I was right, wasn't I? You got it going on. I'd like to see you again.

UNDINE. Why?

GUY. 'Cause I dig you.

UNDINE. You dig me? I am dug. You are seeing me on a good day. You're seeing me way out of context.

GUY. Well, I'm liking what I see.

UNDINE. Oh, so you're going to get smooth? That's okay, bring it, but be warned. I am not an easy person.

GUY. That's cool, but can I see you again?

UNDINE. No, I don't think so. I don't think it's such a good idea.

GUY. Why not?

UNDINE. I can't be with a man in uniform.

GUY. *(Seductively.)* What about a brother out of uniform?

UNDINE. In case you forgot, I'm pregnant.

GUY. So? I think you're brave to make a go of this alone. I got mad respect for you, battling dope, walking the straight and narrow.

UNDINE. It isn't an act of bravery, let me clear that up right now. I didn't plan for this to happen. It is a byproduct of an unholy union.

GUY. And a blessing, no doubt.

UNDINE. You don't let up. You are going to give this a positive spin if it kills you.

GUY. I guess I'm that kinda brother. And I dig that you didn't laugh when I told you about, you know, what I want to do. *(Undine stands up.)*

UNDINE. *(To audience.)* His sincerity is sickening. He has none of Hervé's charm, which makes him all the more charming. Flash forward, a fireman, with a pension and a tacky three-bedroom in Syosset. Flashback, Hervé. *(Hervé, exquisitely attired, appears.)*

HERVÉ. Corfu, Milano, Barcelona, Rio.

UNDINE. *(To audience.)* I am — *(Guy and Hervé retreat into the darkness. Two women in their mid-thirties appear.)*

Scene 2

Courtyard, Walt Whitman projects. Rosa pushes a stroller and wears a Baby Bjorn with an infant. Devora is ghetto fabulous. Undine puts on her sunglasses, trying to avoid contact.

ROSA. *(Shouts.)* SHARONA WATKINS. Sharona!

DEVORA. That can't —

ROSA. Yes, it is.

DEVORA. Oh no, no. *(Undine can't hide.)*

ROSA. Oh hell, somebody told me it was you. But I was, like, what?

UNDINE. Hey.

DEVORA. Hey?

ROSA. You don't remember us, do you?

UNDINE. I'm sorry.

ROSA. *(Sings.)*
     Down, down baby.

ROSA and DEVORA.
     Down by the roller coaster.
     Sweet, sweet baby,
     I'll never let you go.
     Shimmy shimmy coco pop, shimmy, shimmy pop,
     Kissed my boyfriend,

(Undine remembering joins in.)
ALL.
> Naughty, naughty
> Won't do the dishes
> Lazy, Lazy
> Stole a piece of candy
> Greedy, greedy
> Jumped off a building
> Crazy, crazy

(The women laugh.)
UNDINE. The double Dutch twins.
DEVORA. Rosa Ojeda and Devora Williams.
UNDINE. Oh my God. How are you both?
ROSA. I got a little big, but that's what four children and a husband on disability will do.
DEVORA. Don't lie. She's big because —
ROSA. You don't want me to talk about you.
DEVORA. So, Mama. What's up?
UNDINE. I'm … I'm visiting with my parents, while —
DEVORA. For real? How's that fine brother of yours?
UNDINE. He's all right.
DEVORA. Tell him Devora from 2G, said hello. He'll know what you're talking about. Hey!
UNDINE. *(To audience.)* Rosa and Devora were the reigning double Dutch champions in junior high school, but they were eventually beaten by six Japanese girls from Kyoto at Madison Square Garden. It was a crushing blow.
ROSA. I called out to you the other day, but you ain't see me.
UNDINE. I'm sorry. I'm like, you know, dealing with a lot. What are you up to?
ROSA. Not much, you know, the same old, same old. Finally living in building 10, been on the list for seven years. I got me a dope view of Manhattan.
UNDINE. Building 10, no kidding. Congratulations. And Devora? Are you still living in 4?
DEVORA. Oh no. I just bought a brownstone in Fort Greene. I'm a senior financial planner at JP Morgan. I come around once in a while. You know, to see my girl, Rosa. And you? *(A moment.)*
UNDINE. … I'm, um, pregnant and trying —
DEVORA. I bet it's tough, Sharona —
UNDINE. Actually, my name is —

ROSA. That's right, I hear you changed your name to Queen?
UNDINE. No, Undine.
DEVORA. Like Undine Barnes Calles the public relations exec?
UNDINE. I — *(Gregory enters.)*
DEVORA. Pity what happened to her. I hate to see a sister get hurt. I hear she was quite a remarkable diva, but got a little lost. You probably don't even know who I'm talking about. Oh, there's my husband, Gregory. Anyway, it was great seeing you. *(Gregory enters, dressed for success. He waves to the women. Devora starts to leave, but turns back.)* Listen, I'm starting a financial planning program for underprivileged women. Rosa has joined us. I'd love for you to stop by. Here's my card.
UNDINE. *(To audience.)* And as she thrusts the tri-color card into my hand, it gives me a slight paper cut, just enough to draw blood.
DEVORA. Call me.
UNDINE. *(To audience.)* And she means it. *(Devora and Gregory leave.)*
ROSA. She's doing it! And folks like us are just left to sit back and marvel.
UNDINE. But I —
ROSA. I know. Me too. All I gotta say is thank God for social services. It's the Amen at the end of my day. *(Lights rise on a Social Services office, with a line of exhausted people.)*
UNDINE. *(To audience.)* Social services. The most dreaded part of the system.

Scene 3

Department of Social Services. An impatient case worker with long air-brushed nails cradles a phone in her hand, while doing her best to ignore the ever-growing group of people waiting in the endless line. Undine approaches the case worker, and taps on her desk.

CASE WORKER. You don't know how to fill out a form?
UNDINE. I didn't know there was even a form to be filled out.
CASE WORKER. What do the sign say?

UNDINE. Please ill out he orm.

CASE WORKER. So what do that tell you?

UNDINE. Nothing intelligible.

CASE WORKER. Fill this out and come back.

UNDINE. Do I have to wait in line again?

CASE WORKER. Yeah. Next.

UNDINE. But I have already been waiting in line for two hours.

CASE WORKER. Yeah and? I can't do nothing for you until the form's filled out.

UNDINE. Maybe it might be helpful if you let people know that they have to fill out the form before they get to you.

CASE WORKER. Maybe. Next.

UNDINE. Wait. Do I fill out both sides or just the front?

CASE WORKER. Listen, you can rap to me all day, but I ain't like all y'all I got work to do. NEXT.

UNDINE. *(To audience.)* So I meticulously fill out the form. Two hideous hours later. *(The people move in a circular line, until they get back to Undine. Undine walks up to the woman.)* There you go. I was wondering how quickly medical benefits will kick in, you see I'm in a time-sensitive situation —

CASE WORKER. Well, this ain't the right form.

UNDINE. This is the form you gave me.

CASE WORKER. You sure I gave it to you?

UNDINE. Yes.

CASE WORKER. Well, I can't do nothing for you unless you fill out the right form. Next.

UNDINE. Wait just one moment.

PERSON IN LINE. Come on!

UNDINE. What form do I need?

CASE WORKER. 7001.

UNDINE. Which form is this?

CASE WORKER. 7002.

UNDINE. Do you have form 7001?

CASE WORKER. *(Into the phone.)* Hold on, girl. *(The exasperated case worker slams down the telephone. Shouts.)* Lance, you got anymore of form 7001 back there? Bring 'em.

UNDINE. This is crazy. I've been standing in this heat and I — *(Lance hands the case worker a pile of forms.)*

CASE WORKER. You're gonna fill this out and get back in line when you're done.

UNDINE. Excuse me? I'm not waiting another two hours in that line.

CASE WORKER. Then come back first thing tomorrow morning. Next.

WOMAN IN LINE. Don't get too upset. They always like this. I filled out four forms and spent three days here last month. And still ain't got no further then the front desk. In actuality, I don't think there is anything beyond this point. I think that they like to give you the illusion that they can help, keep us busy so we forget that they ain't doing nothing for us.

UNDINE. But don't you want to see what's in the next room?

WOMAN IN LINE. See what's in the next room? *(The woman laughs ironically.)* Good luck ... Send word if you get to the promised land.

UNDINE. *(To case worker.)* I demand to speak to your supervisor.

CASE WORKER. I am the supervisor, what you got to say? *(A moment.)*

UNDINE. Oh? You're the supervisor? Can I say, this whole thing is not being handled professionally. You're rude, and you treat people like cattle. You don't know what circumstances brought each of us here. We've waited all day to get to this point, we just want to sit in a room and talk to somebody, anybody. I mean, isn't there someone in all this miserable bureaucracy who isn't merely concerned with what time to take lunch? We need help. We're entitled to this benefit. We've all humbled ourselves just by being here and you're behaving like some centurion guarding the gates to Rome. I mean, who gave you the right to condescend.

CASE WORKER. And you know what else? We just ran out of the form you need.

UNDINE. He just handed you a pile of forms.

CASE WORKER. So? You think you're entitled to some special treatment. Guess what? I ain't giving you shit. Step out of line until you can stand correct. Next!

WOMAN IN LINE. Oh no, baby, I wouldn't make her angry if I were you.

UNDINE. GIVE ME THE MUTHAFUCKING FORM!

CASE WORKER. Miss, I'll have you medically removed from the building.

UNDINE. I'm not leaving without the form. Give us the form. We want the form. *(Undine urges the others on.)* Come on, people! Give us the form.

OTHERS. *(Chanting.)* We want the form. We want the form. We want the form.

UNDINE. We can come back tomorrow and start this whole damn process again. But who wins?

CROWD. Yeah!

CASE WORKER. NEXT!

UNDINE. *(To audience.)* And I am medically removed from the building, which means the paramedics arrive, administer a mild sedative, strap me to a gurney and rush me to the nearest psychiatric facility. I spend a half hour speaking to a gentle intern who incidentally went to college with my assistant Stephie, and I am subsequently released with a prescription for a powerful antipsychotic ... which I can't use because I'm pregnant. And after all of that I still must go back to the office the next morning to fill out form 7001. And after weeks of agony and bureaucratic hell I was finally able to see a doctor. *(Lights rise on a waiting room in a public medical clinic.)*

Scene 4

Lights shift. We're in a waiting room. A very young pregnant woman sits down next to Undine. The woman noisily sips on a can of grape soda. Undine tries hard to ignore her, finally —

PREGNANT #1. Twins. A boy and girl. The jackpot first time around. What about you?

UNDINE. First.

PREGNANT #1. Your first? Really? But you're so old.

UNDINE. But you're so young. *(A moment. To audience.)* Surely, I don't look that old, do I? *(To her.)* I'm just thirty-seven.

PREGNANT #1. Wow. You're my mother's age.

UNDINE. Your mother is thirty-seven? *(To audience.)* I say nothing, though I want to let her know that I don't belong here, that my life experience is rich and textured and not represented well in this low coarse clinic lighting. As such, I show her a touch of condescension, perhaps even pity. *(Undine displays a touch of condescension. To audience.)* But I'm panicking. *(The young pregnant woman looks at Undine. To audience.)* And I look at her and I realize there, she's

41

looking back at me with a touch of condescension. Pity, even. And we both look away. *(They both look away.)*

PREGNANT#1. My boyfriend is in Iraq.

UNDINE. *(To audience.)* I wish she hadn't told me. *(Undine opens a magazine.)*

PREGNANT #1. I started —

UNDINE. *(To audience.)* She wants to talk, I pretend not to hear her.

PREGNANT #1. We were planning to move out of the —

UNDINE. Please, doctor, call me in. Call me in before Edna returns, I'm having trouble breathing.

PREGNANT #1. I hadn't planned on getting —

UNDINE. Stop! I can't breathe.

PREGNANT #1. I'm scared. *(A moment. Undine reaches out and uncharacteristically takes the pregnant woman's hand.)*

UNDINE. I'm scared too. *(Undine's breathing becomes labored. The lights shifts and we're in the doctor's office.)*

DOCTOR. Ms. Calles. *(Undine stands.)*

UNDINE. Yes.

DOCTOR. Judging from the size of the fetus, I'd predict that you're a little further along than you say.

UNDINE. How much further?

DOCTOR. You're six and a half months.

UNDINE. No, no I can't possibly be that far along.

DOCTOR. That's a conservative estimate. *(The doctor speaks slowly, adopting a patronizing, pedagogic tone.)* I can't impress upon new mothers enough the importance of prenatal care to the health of the fetus. Do you understand what I'm saying?

UNDINE. Doctor, English is my first language, you don't have to speak to me like an idiot. Get to the point.

DOCTOR. Ms. Calles, you really should have come in sooner.

UNDINE. I tried to make an appointment with my regular doctor, but she would no longer see me without health insurance. I attempted to make an appointment with another gynecologist but I needed a referral from the local clinic. I went to the local clinic, but I didn't have the appropriate paperwork. Apparently when I became poor I was no longer worthy of good health care. I don't want —

DOCTOR. If you give this form to the nurse she'll set up your next ultrasound appointment.

UNDINE. No, no, no. You don't understand. I'm not having this baby. No, no, no. I'm not a mother-to-be. Okay. I am not a parent. What can be done?

DOCTOR. At this stage, nothing. You're too far along.

UNDINE. Yeah, but what can be done?

DOCTOR. Eat right and take good care of yourself. Here's a prescription for prenatal vitamins. I'll see you in a month. *(The doctor passes Undine the prescription.)* Oh, Ms. Calles, would you like to hear the baby's heartbeat before you leave?

UNDINE. What?

DOCTOR. Many women like —

UNDINE. No … yes. I'm not sure. *(A moment.)* Doctor.

DOCTOR. Yes?

UNDINE. Do you think the baby knows what I'm feeling?

DOCTOR. I don't know. But I like to think so. *(A moment. The doctor exits. Undine sits, frozen. She looks at the prescription.)*

UNDINE. *(Contemplating, to audience.)* Optimox prenatal tabs? I go to Duane Reade on the Upper West Side, it's like a vacation wandering the well-stocked aisles of the pharmacy with employees in pristine uniforms. *(Lights shift, we're in Duane Reade. Pleasant music plays in the back ground.)*

Scene 5

Duane Reade. A young woman, dressed in a uniform, busies herself stocking items on a shelf.

UNDINE. Miss. I'm looking for calcium tablets and vitamins. *(Stephie, startled, turns around in her pharmacy uniform.)* Stephie?

STEPHIE. Undine? *(They gawk at each other.)*

UNDINE. What are —

STEPHIE. This is only temporary. Actually I'm interviewing like crazy. I've come really close to several things. God, look at you.

UNDINE. Look at you.

STEPHIE. I tried to call you last month for a recommendation, but —

UNDINE. I've moved to Brooklyn.

STEPHIE. Great.

UNDINE. It's great.

STEPHIE. Great.

43

UNDINE. Great. *(A moment.)*

STEPHIE. This is about paying a few bills. I'm told it's like important to have all kinds of experiences.

UNDINE. True.

STEPHIE. Man. How far along are you?

UNDINE. Seven months.

STEPHIE. You with a baby. *(Stephie gives off a little laugh.)*

UNDINE. Why is that funny to you?

STEPHIE. I don't know. I'm sorry, but you always seemed like —

UNDINE. Like what?

STEPHIE. I don't know. Like. *(A moment.)* Never mind.

UNDINE. The calcium pills are in which aisle?

STEPHIE. Seven, no, no. Four. I'm trying not to get used to this. I don't really want to know where things are, because once you do, you sorta committed. Right? This is just temporary.

LOUDSPEAKER. Stephie, you're needed in aisle two, for stacking.

STEPHIE. Oh God they're calling me. I'm like the stock guru. If I really wanted to, I could be employee of the month, every month. But there's nothing worse than bad blood between minimum wage workers. I'm not trying to go there.

LOUDSPEAKER. Stephie, you're needed in aisle two. Pronto!

STEPHIE. Coming! Like nothing changes. I gotta run.

UNDINE. Go. *(Stephie turns to leave.)*

STEPHIE. Hey Undine. Undine! Are you happy? *(Undine turns away.)*

UNDINE. *(To audience.)* I want to turn back, but I don't. I do not answer. I slip the calcium tablets into my pocket, unpaid, and I keep walking. I walk all the way home. *(Crossfade to —)*

Scene 6

Kitchen table. Flow and Mother, as usual, are dressed in their security guard uniforms. They are in the midst of a conversation. Grandma is crocheting a doily. Mother is sweeping the floor. Undine, ankles swollen, navigates the kitchen table trying to find a comfortable place to sit. The pregnancy is intruding on her life. She is breathing with difficulty.

FLOW. And I took the shoplifter to back of the store and gave him my Nelson Mandela speech. I said, "The African brother gave up twenty-eight years of freedom for his ideals, for his principles, for the struggle to liberate Black Africans from the grip-lock of apartheid." I said, "Little brother thief, liberating a box of lubricated super-strong Trojans ain't a reason to go to jail. Don't let the system fuck you because you're horny. If you're going to give up your damn free-dom, make sure it's for a just cause." And, Ma, I saw a little some-thing in his eyes, a spark, a touch of recognition, and I quickly unfas-tened his handcuffs. And then this little fool is gonna ask, "Who Nelson Mandela?" I had to slap homeboy out of his chair and call 911. Shit, there ain't no greater crime than abandoning your history.

MOTHER. That's right. *(Undine is breathing heavily, struggles with the child-resistant container of calcium tablets.)*

UNDINE. Hello, could someone give me hand?

MOTHER. Flow! *(Flow helps Undine lower herself into a kitchen chair. She lands with an audible thud.)*

FLOW. Damn girl, you getting big.

UNDINE. What-ever.

FLOW. Sharona!

UNDINE. Ty-rell!

FLOW. Here's a little something for the baby daddy. *(Flow does a series of elaborate tricks with his billy club. Undine grabs the club and places it on the table.)*

MOTHER. You two are acting like teenagers. Stop it. Oh Undine, somebody called for you while you were at the doctor's office.

UNDINE. Who?

FLOW. Did you tell them there ain't no Undine living here?

UNDINE. That's getting old, okay.

FLOW. What's the matter with you?

UNDINE. What's the matter with me? I'm almost forty and liv-ing at home and believe it or not I envy the fact that my assistant Stephie is employee of the month at Duane Reade. Okay? Mom, did the phone call sound important?

MOTHER. I don't know, what does important sound like?

UNDINE. *(To audience.)* A pardon. Absolution. My life back. Was it Hervé calling from Barbados to say "join me"? Would I? Would I?

MOTHER. I'm sure they'll call back. *(Father, seemingly tired, enters wearing security uniform.)*

FLOW. Hey there. What's the word, Pop?

MOTHER. Hope you didn't forget the Lotto tickets … Don't tell me you forgot.

FATHER. I forgot? *(Excited.)* I ain't forget. *(Father drops a pile of Lotto receipts on the table. He gives Mother a kiss on the head.)* The Lotto line ran around the block. Stood, twenty-five minutes. Junie got heself one hundred tickets, he thinks this time he gonna be lucky 'cause Clarice Momma had a dream about fish. But he doesn't want to share his luck with anybody, jack.

UNDINE. Mom, Mom was it a man that called?

MOTHER. Did she really dream about fish?

FLOW. When that woman dream fish, money fall out the sky?

UNDINE. Fish?

FLOW. Don't you know, girl? *(Grandma, suddenly.)*

GRANDMA. It means good fortune coming your way. It's a sacred kiss, sweet pea. *(Mother suddenly remembers.)*

MOTHER. Oh that's right, it was a man that called, Grandma said —

UNDINE. You let him speak to Grandma?

MOTHER. I had a pot of gumbo about to burn on the stove.

FATHER. You made your gumbo?

UNDINE. *(Exasperated.)* Grandma, was it my accountant? Was it … Hervé?

GRANDMA. Who's Hervé?

UNDINE. He's my husband. What did the man say? It's very important! *(Shouts.)* I need to know!

FLOW. Don't you yell at her! She's an old woman! She's got diabetes, damn it.

UNDINE. Flow, she doesn't have diabetes. For God's sake, I've been taking her to the methadone clinic for a month. People! Hello! *(Shouts.)* Is anybody home?

MOTHER. Why are you so upset? It's just a phone call. If it's important the person will call back.

UNDINE. It isn't the phone call! It's … It's a phantom poem that won't ever be completed, it's thousands of dollars of Lotto tickets that should have been invested in the stock market, it's a thrown-away solution and, Mom, you're still searching for words, it's the fact that Grandma can be a —

GRANDMA. She's carry low. It makes some people crazy, in the third trimester.

UNDINE. Aren't you listening to what I'm saying? Or are we just going to sit around all day and talk about fish. *(A moment. Flow*

suddenly jumps up. He beats out a rhythm with his night stick.)
FLOW. *(Furious passion.)*

    This ain't the beginnin' you wuz expectin'
    It ain't a poem, but a reckonin'
    Be it sacred or profane,
    Or a divine word game.
    It all about a rabbit,
    Or it ain't.

    It ain't a holler or a song.
    It ain't no geechie folk yawn.
    It ain't a road that been tread,
    With a stained rag around the head.
    It all about a rabbit,
    Or ain't.

    It ain't a myth that so old,
    That it been wholesaled and resold.
    It ain't a bible lovers' tale
    Or a preacher's parting wail.

    Wait. Wait. Okay. Here we go.
    It all about a rabbit,
    Or ain't.

    'Cuz.

    It that ghetto paradox,
    When we rabbit and we fox.
    And we basking in the blight
    Though we really wanna fight.

    It 'bout who we be today
    And in our fabulating way.
    'bout saying that we be
    without a-pology.
    It's a circle that been run
    That ain't no one ever won.
    It that silly rabbit grin.
    'bout running from your skin,

'Cuz.

It a ... It a ...
MOTHER. C'mon.
FLOW. It a ... It ... *(Flow stops middle sentence as abruptly as he began, struggling to find the next verse in the poem.)*
FATHER. Don't stop —
FLOW. But, it ain't finished. It ain't done 'til it's done. A fabulation takes time. It doesn't just happen.
UNDINE. A Fabulation? Yeah, but how long, Flow?
FLOW. I don't know, fourteen years and nine months. What do you care? We died in a fire. *(A moment.)*
UNDINE. *(To audience.)* It was an unforeseen tragedy, really. A misprint.
MOTHER. We saw the article in *Black Enterprise*.
FATHER. We ain't totally blind. We read. Your grandma didn't want —
MOTHER. It was a very good article, Undine. We were very proud of you, until the part where they said your family died in a fire. Baby, we didn't die in a fire.
UNDINE. Yes, I know that. I was apparently misquoted.
FLOW. A misquote?
MOTHER. That's what I told your father. You see, baby. I told him that. I said she's done many things, but she'd never do that.
FATHER. Is that true ... Undine?
UNDINE. Surely, you can't believe everything you read.
FLOW. WHY?
FATHER. We are your family! The Watkins family is there inside you. And we gonna love it, even if ... This *is* your home.
UNDINE. *(To audience.)* Is this it? Is this the end of the story? Is it that simple? A journey that began miraculously at the Walt Whitman projects and led me to Edith Wharton's *The Custom of the Country*, an intriguing parvenu discovered in an American Literature course at Dartmouth College. *(A moment.)* No. No. I go to a street corner with a twenty-dollar bill balled up in my hand. I buy twenty dollars' worth of white lace. I take it home. I really must have angered Elegba, I must have unsettled all of the powerful orishas. And I'm ready to surrender, I'm ready, to concede, I'm so ready and just as I'm about ... they unexpectedly find Hervé. *(A prison waiting room.)*

Scene 7

Hervé slowly emerges from the darkness wearing a bright orange prison uniform; he moves with grace. Undine sits across from him at the prison visitor's table.

UNDINE. They found him hiding out at the Ritz-Carlton pretending to be a diplomat from Uruguay, unfortunately for him a diplomat from Uruguay was also a guest at the hotel attending a summit on global warming. Caught, finally. *(Hervé points to her bulging stomach.)*

HERVÉ. What happened to you?

UNDINE. What do you think happened to me?

HERVÉ. Who did this to you?

UNDINE. You did, you fucker!

HERVÉ. Me?

UNDINE. Yes. *(A moment.)*

HERVÉ. How?

UNDINE. How do you think?

HERVÉ. Yes, I see. *(A moment.)*

UNDINE. Why?

HERVÉ. Why not?

UNDINE. All of it?

HERVÉ. It happened, *si.* It is finished.

UNDINE. I could kill you. I cared for you, you little prick. And you didn't even have the decency to say goodbye.

HERVÉ. I am sorry.

UNDINE. You can take your sorry to federal prison.

HERVÉ. Let us talk.

UNDINE. I have nothing to say to you. My lawyer will speak for me. You took everything from me.

HERVÉ. Not everything. My father's name was Javier Dejesus Calles. He was a good man. I offer you his name, it is the name for my son, for my daughter.

UNDINE. Well, that won't do.

HERVÉ. But, I am the father of your child.

UNDINE. Oh please, you were fucking for a green card, that's

49

enough to keep any Latin dick hard. *(A moment.)* You are the father, but you won't be this child's father. You left our lives, you gave up your parental rights as far as I am concerned. I was generous to you, I was more than generous.

HERVÉ. I beg your pardon, *querida* you were generous to nobody. I disappeared long before I left, but you just never noticed. Money, you'll make more money. Don't pretend it was about the money.

UNDINE. Oh please.

HERVÉ. I pity the child.

UNDINE. Why would you say that?

HERVÉ. I think you understand, Undine. *(Undine stares at Hervé.)* I was open, but you are a rotten oyster. We look at each other, now. It is the first time we stand face to face since we met, no? I am who I was, *querida*, you are who you were. We are ugly people. We give, we take, we are even.

UNDINE. *(To audience.)* I've prided myself on not needing love, but it was different when I thought I was loved.

HERVÉ. Guard. *(Hervé leaves.)*

UNDINE. *(Resigned.)* Hervé! *(To audience.)* And he is gone. But strangely I dream of fish. *(The sound of the ocean. Undine is surrounded by the group of addicts.)*

Scene 8

The addicts sit in a support circle, Undine and Guy are seated close to each other.

ADDICT #2. Old friends, old friends. I shouldn't have rode in the car with my old friends, they were smoking herb and I thought, a little herb won't kill me.

COUNSELOR. Take a moment. We're not here to judge, this is a place of forgiveness. Take your time. *(Addict #2 begins to weep. Undine lets out a loud involuntary gasp.)* Are you okay, Undine?

UNDINE. Yes. I'm sorry.

GUY. *(Whispered.)* Did you get my telephone message?

UNDINE. You? No.

GUY. No? *(Whispers.)* Have you begun your birthing classes?

UNDINE. *(Whispered.)* I haven't even thought that far ahead.

GUY. Don't you think maybe you better?

UNDINE. Yes. I suppose eventually I will have to give birth.

GUY. If you need someone to go with you to the classes, I'd be glad.

UNDINE. That's okay.

COUNSELOR. Was there something you wish to share with the group, Undine?

UNDINE. Oh no.

ADDICT #2. The radio was pumping, the feeling was familiar. Two hits, what's the harm?

GUY. *(Whispered.)* Really, if you need a partner, someone to be in the delivery room with you. I know we don't know each other that well, and I don't want to make you uncomfortable. But I'd be happy to be that person that you know, stands by you in the delivery room.

UNDINE. Really?

GUY. Yeah.

ADDICT #2. I'm trying to be mindful. I will no longer inhabit the places of my past. *(The circle applauds.)*

UNDINE. You'll hold my hand? Breathe in and out with me?

GUY. I am serious.

UNDINE. Yes, I know that you're serious and yes, I would like for you to be that person who stands by me in the ... delivery room. Oh my god, this is going to happen.

GUY. You ain't like the other addicts in this program. I mean you seem ... stronger.

UNDINE. *(To audience.)* But he doesn't know that Edna is pressing gently against my chest, slowly quickening my breath, squeezing. *(Undine touches her swollen belly.)* Or that I feel the child kicking within, the tiny left foot jabbing at my side, stretching, growing, causing unbearable, intolerable pain. The contradictions abound, my body is no longer my own. *(Guy, smiling, gently places his hand on Undine's belly.)*

GUY. Hey.

UNDINE. Why are you smiling?

GUY. You.

UNDINE. What?

GUY. You know.

UNDINE. Yes?

GUY. Look beautiful.

UNDINE. No.

GUY. I am happy.

UNDINE. Happy?

GUY. Yes. I am happy.

UNDINE. Truly?

GUY. Yeah, you make me happy. It has been a struggle, no doubt, but when I think about what's happened to me in the last few months, it's good, for real. You. Three years ago I was living on the street, five blocks away from where I grew up. I'd see my moms, my boys and they'd pretend not to know me. I was starving, and they'd walk right by me. Ashamed. Yeah, I been that person. I been that brother you cross the street to avoid, I been wrong at times, I been to jail for six months. But that's over, never again. I let go of the bullshit. I hope you know that. Why do you look confused?

UNDINE. I've never heard anyone say, "I'm happy," and actually feel it. People around me say it automatically in response to "How are you doing?" But when you say it, I'm looking at you, I believe you actually mean it. And I find that reassuring. *(The addicts slowly shift their attention to Undine and Guy.)*

GUY. Why?

UNDINE. Because mostly I feel rage. *(Undine realizes the addicts are eavesdropping and finds herself including them in her confessional.)* Anger, which I guess is a variation of rage and sometimes it gives way to panic, which in my case is also a variation of rage. I think it's safe to say that I have explored the full range of rage. And it has been with me for so long, that it's comforting. I'm trying to move beyond it, sometimes I even think I have, but mostly I'm not a very good human being. Sometimes I'm less than human, I know this, but I can't control it. I killed my family. *(A collective gasp.)* Yes, I killed them. It was on the day of my college graduation. Dartmouth. My family drove 267 miles in a rented minivan, loaded with friends and relatives eager to witness my ceremony. They were incredibly proud, and why not? I was the first person in the family to graduate from college. They came en masse, dressed in their Alexander's best. Loud, overly eager, lugging picnic baskets filled with fragrant ghetto food … let's just say their enthusiasm overwhelmed me. But I didn't mind, no, I didn't mind until I over-heard a group of my friends making crass unkind comments about my family. They wondered aloud who belonged to *those* people. It was me. I should have said so. I should have said that my mother took an extra shift so I could have a new coat every year. My father sent me ten dollars every week, his Lotto money. But instead I locked myself in my dorm room and refused to come out to greet them. And I decided on that day, that I was Undine Barnes, who bore no relationship to those people. I told everyone my family died in a fire, and I came to accept it as true. It was true for years. Understand, Sharona had to die in a fire in order for Undine to live. At least that's what I thought. What I did was awful, and I'm so so sorry. And, Guy, you are such a good, decent man. And I wouldn't blame you if you walked away right now. But I don't want you to. I feel completely safe with you.

GUY. That is a good thing.

UNDINE. I am not yet divorced, I'm being investigated by the FBI, I'm carrying the child of another man and I'm not really a junkie. *(A collective gasp from the addicts.)* Are you still happy?

GUY. Yes, I think so.

UNDINE. And you're not medicated?

GUY. No.

UNDINE. Give us a moment. *(A moment. Undine pulls Guy aside.)* Is the notion of love frightening to you?

GUY. No.

UNDINE. Who are you? Why are you doing this? I'm sorry, I didn't mean to say that. I take it back. I mean, I like you a great deal. Love is heavy, is deep and frightening and I apologize for floating it so carelessly. I really want to change, I do, but I'm afraid I can't. I'm not ready for this.

GUY. Stop. Stop speaking. *(Guy leans in and plants a kiss on Undine's lips; she surrenders. A labor pain hits. The addicts gasp)*

Scene 9

Lights slowly shift to birthing room. Guy helps Undine onto the examining table. Bright, unforgiving light. Undine sits on the birth table.

UNDINE. *(To audience.)* A child? *(Panic.)* My child. *(Guy smiles. A pain strikes, interrupting Undine's words.)*

GUY. Breathe. *(Undine lies down on the delivery table.)*

UNDINE. *(To audience.)* Everyone wants me to breathe out, push, but I am trying desperately to hold my breath, hold it in. If

I don't breathe then the baby will not come.

GUY. Breathe, Undine.

UNDINE. *(To audience.)* I am holding my breath.

DOCTOR. Breathe.

UNDINE. *(To audience.)* I am holding on. *(Undine refuses to breathe, Guy takes her hand.)*

GUY. Please, breathe.

UNDINE. *(To audience.)* I won't. I won't a bring a child into this world. *(Grandma, Mother, Father, Flow enter wearing their security guard uniforms.)*

FLOW. Breathe, girl!

MOTHER and FATHER. Breathe, Undine!

GRANDMA. Breathe, sweet pea! *(Undine looks at her family and Guy in their uniforms, then at their concerned faces.)*

UNDINE. *(To audience.)* And then I let go. *(Undine wails, a tremendous release. Silence. To audience.)* I breathe. *(A baby cries. Blackout.)*

End of Play

PROPERTY LIST

Cigarette and lighter/matches
Telephone headset (UNDINE)
Hand mirror (UNDINE)
Lipstick (UNDINE)
Papers (ACCOUNTANT)
Cocktail (HERVÉ)
Medical chart (DR. KHDAIR)
Broccoli spear (HERVÉ)
Napkin (HERVÉ)
Two glasses (ALLISON)
Bottle of wine (ALLISON)
Daily News (ALLISON, FATHER)
Office equipment MOVERS)
Candle (YORUBA PRIEST)
Nigerian divination board (YORUBA PRIEST)
Cowrie shells (YORUBA PRIEST)
Crochet needles (GRANDMA)
Doily (GRANDMA)
Paper bag containing baggie of white powder, box of matches,
 hypodermic needle, spoon, tourniquet (UNDINE)
Cup of hot chocolate (MOTHER)
Money (UNDINE)
Bag (UNDINE)
Gucci sunglasses (UNDINE)
Cup of coffee (UNDINE)
Stroller (ROSA)
Baby Bjorn with infant (ROSA)
Business card (DEVORA)
Phone (CASE WORKER)
Forms (CASE WORKER, LANCE)
Can of grape soda (PREGNANT, #1)
Magazine (UNDINE)
Prescription (DOCTOR)
Broom (MOTHER)
Bottle of calcium tablets (UNDINE)
Billy club (FLOW)
Lotto receipts (FATHER)

SOUND EFFECTS

Slow tango
Police sirens
Pleasant music
Baby crying